AI FOR EVERYONE: A BEGINNER-FRIENDLY GUIDE FOR UNDERSTANDING ARTIFICIAL INTELLIGENCE

Simplify AI Concepts to Inspire Your Journey from Curious Beginner to Confident User

"Any sufficiently advanced technology is indistinguishable from magic." — Arthur C. Clarke

CONTENTS

INTRODUCTION: WELCOME TO THE WORLD OF AI

The Purpose of This Book

Artificial intelligence, or AI, is no longer just a concept from sci-fi movies or high-tech research labs. It's all around us, powering the apps on your phone, customizing your shopping lists, and even helping doctors diagnose illnesses. Yet, AI often seems hidden behind complex terms and confusing processes. That's where this book comes in.

The aim here is simple: to make AI easy to understand and accessible for everyone. You don't need to be a tech expert. This book will guide you step by step through what AI is and how it works. By the end, you'll not only understand the basics of AI, but you'll also feel confident exploring how it can enhance your work, business, or personal projects.

AI is transforming our world, and it's already a part of your daily life, whether you notice it or not. But learning about AI isn't just about keeping up with trends; it's about empowering yourself. Have you ever wondered how your phone seems to know exactly what you're interested in? Understanding AI is like learning a new language... one that opens up a world of possibilities. You're not just a bystander in this transformation; you're an active participant, ready to use these tools to your advantage.

What is Artificial Intelligence?

Let's dive into the big question: What exactly is AI? At its heart, AI is about machines doing tasks that usually need human smarts. This includes things like understanding speech, making decisions, learning from data, and even coming up with creative ideas. If that sounds complicated, don't worry... it's much simpler once we break it down.

Think of it this way: each time you ask Siri or

Alexa about the weather, AI is at work. When Netflix recommends a movie you end up loving, that's also AI. It's not magic; it's technology based on patterns and data. While AI can sometimes seem mysterious, this book aims to open that mystery box and show you what's inside—*without all the intimidating jargon and tech talk, right?* Let's explore it together, step by step!

How to Use This Book

This book is your guide to understanding AI, and like any good guide, it's here to take you on a journey. Whether you're brand new to AI or you've tried a few apps and tools, this book will meet you where you are and help you build a solid foundation.

Here's what you can expect:

Chapter 1: The Basics of AI

We'll kick things off with the essentials—what AI is, how it works, and the many ways it's already influencing the world around us. By the end of this chapter, you'll have a clear understanding of the building blocks of AI and how they come together.

Chapter 2: Understanding AI's Potential and

Limitations

We'll explore what AI can and can't do. This chapter will help you separate the hype from reality, offering a balanced view of its capabilities and challenges.

Chapter 3: Getting Started with AI Tools**

Finally, we'll dive into practical applications. You'll discover AI tools you can start using today, whether for personal productivity, creative projects, or professional goals. This chapter is all about setting you up to take action with what you've learned.

Each chapter is broken into bite-sized sections with clear explanations, real examples, and "next steps" to get you started. You don't need to read the whole book in one go—feel free to jump around or revisit sections as you need. Think of this book as a friendly chat with someone excited to share what they know about AI.

Along the way, you'll find tips for applying AI concepts in real life, whether you want to streamline your workday, launch a new project, or simply keep up with this rapidly changing field. The goal isn't just to teach you about AI—it's to show you how to use it in ways that make sense for you.

By the end of this book, you'll have moved from Point A—someone who knows little or nothing about AI—to Point B—someone who's confident in the basics and ready to start exploring its possibilities. So, take a deep breath, relax, and let's set off on this journey together. The world of AI is waiting for you!

**Bonus Guide: TheAivilleExpert.com

From your Author...

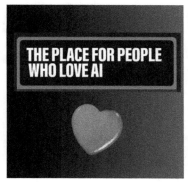

As someone who's diving deep into the world of AI, I want to introduce you to a special *"Place for People Who Love AI."* You'll find this magical place at "TheAiVilleExpert.com."

Copy and paste this link into your favorite browser, and you'll be whisked away to a vibrant online community where everything AI is right at your fingertips. It's a cozy, friendly space for people just like you. Whether you're a curious newcomer or a seasoned expert, this is the perfect gateway to a universe of AI possibilities, including networking, AI jobs, tools, educational courses, and more.

Join over 5,000 members who are already part of this thriving AI community. And the best part? You can start for free...check it out! Just so you know, I am a paid member myself.

On the right below, you'll see Mattie, one of the AI char

acters I created using ChatGPT. I brought Mattie to life in an Instagram Reel that shares more about our AI community. I used Eleven Labs to give Mattie a voice and D-ID Studios to animate her.

I started this video reel from scratch, with no prior experience. You can do it, too. Check out what Mattie has to say about our special community on: Instagram.com/TheAiVilleExpert/

CHAPTER 1: THE BASICS OF AI

What Exactly is AI?

The begics of   AI
The basics of Acr beginners
ORIGINAL ORIGINAL

Let's kick off our journey by uncovering the essence of this topic: What exactly is artificial intelligence? The term "AI" often brings to mind futuristic robots or computers that think like humans, but the reality is both simpler and more fascinating. At its heart, AI is about machines imitating certain aspects of human intelligence to do tasks that usually need human effort. These tasks can range from recognizing patterns and making predictions to solving problems and even creating art. To truly understand AI, it's helpful to explore its definitions, its history, and the foundational concepts that make it tick.

Definitions and Types of AI

Artificial intelligence, in its simplest terms, refers to a machine's ability to perform tasks that usually require human intelligence. This can include recognizing speech, analyzing data, or making decisions. However, not all AI is created equal, and understanding its different types helps clarify what AI can do.

The most common type of AI we encounter is called narrow AI, and it's what we interact with every day. Narrow AI is designed to perform a specific task, and it does this remarkably well. For instance, the recommendation algorithms that suggest movies on Netflix or products on Amazon are examples of narrow AI. They excel in their domain, but they can't step outside of it. Your Netflix algorithm, for example, won't help you navigate traffic or predict the weather.

Then there's general AI, the type of AI that, for now, exists only in science fiction. General AI would be able to perform any intellectual task that a human can do, learning and adapting across various fields. While researchers dream of creating such systems, today's AI focuses on excelling in specialized areas rather than mimicking human cognition across the board.

In practical terms, AI is already woven into the fabric of our lives. From smartphones and smart home devices to algorithms that help doctors make better diagnoses, AI is everywhere. The key is understanding that while AI can be incredibly powerful, it's a tool designed to assist and enhance human efforts, not replace them.

The History of AI

To understand where AI stands today, it helps to look back at its origins. The concept of intelligent machines isn't new. It dates back to ancient myths and dreams of creating life through mechanical means. However, AI as a field of study truly began in the mid-20th century.

In 1950, Alan Turing, often referred to as the father of modern computing, asked a groundbreaking question: "Can machines think?" His work laid the groundwork for AI by exploring whether machines could simulate human thought. Just a few years later, in 1956, the term "artificial intelligence" was coined during a conference at Dartmouth College, marking the start of AI as an academic discipline.

The early days of AI focused on tasks that required logical reasoning, such as solving mathematical problems or playing games. Over time, the field grew to include learning and pattern recognition. Major milestones followed, like IBM's Deep Blue defeating world chess champion Garry Kasparov in 1997, and Google's AlphaGo mastering the ancient game of Go in 2016. Each achievement showed that AI could handle increasingly complex challenges.

The history of AI isn't just about machines; it's also about people. Visionaries like Turing, John McCarthy, and Marvin Minsky laid the foundation for the field, while modern innovators continue to expand its horizons. Understanding this history reveals that AI has always been driven by the human desire to solve problems and explore new possibilities.

Core Concepts of AI

At its core, AI is about teaching machines to think and learn, albeit in ways that differ from human intelligence. Three key concepts—machine learning, deep learning, and neural networks—form the backbone of how AI functions.

Machine learning is perhaps the most fundamental

concept. It allows machines to learn from data without being explicitly programmed for every situation. Imagine teaching a computer to recognize handwritten numbers. Instead of programming rules for every possible way a "3" might appear, you feed the computer thousands of examples. Over time, it learns the patterns and can identify new examples on its own.

Deep learning takes this idea further by using complex structures called neural networks, which are inspired by how the human brain processes information. These networks excel at tasks like image and speech recognition. For instance, when your phone recognizes your face to unlock, it uses deep learning to match your facial features to the stored data.

Neural networks are a fascinating piece of technology. They consist of layers of interconnected nodes, with each layer processing information and passing it along to the next. Each node evaluates the data, figuring out which features are important for making a decision. For example, when deciding if a photo contains a dog or a cat, different nodes might focus on fur texture, ear shape, or eye size. The final layer brings all this information together to make a prediction.

These concepts—machine learning, deep learning, and neural networks—might sound complex, but they all boil down to this: enabling machines to recognize patterns and make informed decisions. With these tools, AI can perform tasks that once seemed reserved for humans, like diagnosing diseases or composing music.

With these foundational elements in place, you now have a clear understanding of what AI is, where it originated, and the principles that make it work. This is the first step in your journey to understanding and applying AI in your own life. Next, we'll explore how AI works behind the scenes, diving deeper into the role of data, algorithms, and the hardware that powers it.

How AI Works

AI might seem like magic, but it's all about the careful combination of data, algorithms, and computing power. Every AI system depends on these three core elements working together to perform tasks, learn from experience, and improve over time. To understand this process, we'll explore the role of data, the workings of algorithms and models, and the hardware that drives these systems.

The Role of Data in AI

Data is the foundation of any AI system. It's the raw material that machines process to learn patterns, make predictions, and perform tasks. Imagine trying to bake a cake without ingredients... that's what AI would be like without data. But it's not just about having data; it's about having the right data.

We live in the era of "big data," where we generate enormous amounts of information every second. Consider the texts you send, the photos you share, or even the steps you track with a fitness app. All of this contributes to a vast pool of data that AI can analyze. For example, when you open your favorite music streaming app, AI sifts through billions of data points from users worldwide to recommend songs you're likely to enjoy. The more data AI has, the better it becomes at spotting patterns and making accurate predictions.

But having a lot of data isn't enough—it needs to be high-quality data. Poor-quality data can lead to inaccurate results, often described by the phrase "garbage in, garbage out." For instance, if an AI system designed to detect fraudulent transactions is trained on incomplete or biased data, it may incorrectly flag legitimate transactions as suspicious or overlook actual fraud. This is why data preparation, like cleaning and organizing information, is a crucial step in AI development.

AI doesn't just use data—it learns from it. By analyzing historical data, AI systems can make decisions or predictions about new situations. For example, a self-driving car collects real-time data from its surroundings—such as traffic patterns, road conditions, and nearby vehicles—to navigate safely. Without data, none of this would be possible.

Algorithms and Models

While data is the fuel for AI, algorithms are the engine. An algorithm is essentially a set of rules or instructions that tells a machine how to process data and make decisions. In AI, algorithms are used to create models, which act as the brains of the system.

Think of an algorithm as a recipe and the AI model as the finished dish. When you train an AI model, you're feeding data into an algorithm so it can learn patterns and rules. For example, to train a model to recognize emails as spam or not spam, you'd provide it with thousands of examples. The algorithm analyzes these examples, identifying common traits in spam emails, such as specific phrases or unusual formatting. Over time, the model becomes skilled at distinguishing between spam and legitimate emails.

Different algorithms have different purposes. Linear regression, for example, is used for making predictions, like forecasting next month's sales based on past trends. Decision trees help AI systems make choices by breaking down data into a series of if-then questions. Then there are neural networks, which mimic how the human brain processes information, and are used for tasks like recognizing faces or translating languages.

Once a model is trained, it can make decisions or predictions with new data. For example, weather forecasting AI might use its trained model to predict tomorrow's temperature based on today's conditions. The more data the model encounters, the better it becomes at refining its predictions. This process of learning and improving is what makes AI so powerful.

The Role of Hardware

All this data processing and algorithm training requires significant computing power, and that's where hardware comes in. Without the right hardware, AI wouldn't be able to manage the vast amounts of data or the complex calculations it needs.

Graphics processing units, or GPUs, are the workhorses of AI. Originally designed for rendering graphics in video games, GPUs have become essential for AI because they can handle large volumes of data simultaneously. For example, when you ask your smartphone's voice assistant a question, GPUs help process your voice input and generate a response in real-time.

In addition to GPUs, many AI systems rely on cloud computing. This means that instead of being limited to a single computer, data and algorithms are stored and processed on remote servers. Cloud computing allows AI to scale up, managing huge tasks like analyzing global weather patterns or training complex language models. Services like Google Translate, for example, use cloud computing to process your text input and deliver accurate translations within seconds.

As technology advances, specialized hardware is being developed specifically for AI tasks. AI chips, for instance, are designed to optimize tasks like image recognition and natural language processing. Quantum computing, although still in its early stages, holds the promise of revolutionizing AI by performing calculations at speeds far beyond today's capabilities. These innovations ensure that AI systems will continue to grow faster, smarter, and more efficient.

By combining data, algorithms, and hardware, AI works behind the scenes to power the systems we rely on every day. Now that you understand the mechanics of how AI functions, let's explore the many ways AI is applied in the real world. From streamlining daily tasks to transforming entire industries, the applications of AI today are truly remarkable.

Applications for AI Today

AI is everywhere, even if you don't always notice it. From the apps on your phone to systems that streamline businesses and industries, AI has seamlessly woven itself into our daily lives. In this section, we'll explore the practical ways AI is used today, breaking it down into everyday life, business applications, and specialized industries.

AI in Everyday Life

When you wake up in the morning and check your phone, AI is already hard at work. Take your email app, for example—AI filters out spam, keeping your inbox free of unwanted messages. As you scroll through social media, you'll notice posts tailored to your interests, thanks to algorithms analyzing your behavior and preferences. This is AI in action, making your experience more personalized and engaging.

Voice assistants like Alexa, Siri, and Google Assistant have become household staples, capable of setting reminders, playing music, or even answering trivia questions. These tools rely on natural language processing, a branch of AI that helps machines understand and respond to human speech. Similarly, AI powers your favorite streaming platforms, like Netflix or Spotify, recommending shows or songs based on your past preferences.

AI even enhances your morning commute. Navigation apps like Google Maps use machine learning to analyze traffic patterns and suggest the quickest routes. If you're using a ridesharing app like Uber, AI matches you with nearby drivers and calculates the optimal route to your destination. By the time you start your day, you've already interacted with AI multiple times without even realizing it.

AI in Business

AI is transforming the way businesses operate, making them more efficient, productive, and customer-focused. One of the most visible applications is in customer service. Chatbots, powered by AI, manage basic inquiries, freeing up human agents to handle more complex issues. These bots are available 24/7, ensuring customers always have support, whether it's for tracking a package or troubleshooting a product.

In marketing, AI is a game-changer. Tools like predictive analytics allow businesses to anticipate customer needs and tailor their strategies accordingly. For instance, online retailers use AI to recommend products you're likely to buy based on your browsing and purchase history. This not only enhances customer satisfaction but also boosts sales.

AI also streamlines behind-the-scenes operations. In supply chain management, AI helps predict demand, optimize inventory, and identify potential disruptions. Similarly, in finance, AI systems analyze market trends and assess risks, enabling faster and more informed decision-making. These applications show how businesses use AI not just to improve their bottom line but also to enhance the overall customer experience.

AI in Specialized Industries

Beyond everyday and business use, AI is making groundbreaking strides in specialized fields, transforming industries like healthcare, education, and the arts. In healthcare, AI is saving lives. It's used to analyze medical images, helping doctors detect diseases like cancer at earlier stages. AI-powered tools also assist in creating personalized treatment plans, ensuring patients receive care tailored to their specific needs.

In education, AI enhances learning effectiveness. Personalized learning platforms adapt to individual learning styles, offering customized content and feedback. This approach helps struggling students catch up and challenges advanced learners to reach their full potential. AI tutors are becoming more common, providing one-on-one assistance outside the traditional classroom setting.

Even creative industries are embracing AI. In art, AI tools like DALL-E and MidJourney enable artists to generate stunning visuals from simple text descriptions. Musicians use AI to compose original scores, while writers leverage AI for brainstorming ideas or improving their drafts. Far from replacing human creativity, these tools enhance it, acting as collaborators in the creative process.

The applications of AI today are as diverse as they are transformative, impacting nearly every aspect of our lives. From simplifying daily tasks to revolutionizing industries, AI's potential is vast and ever-growing. Now that you've seen how AI is being applied, it's time to explore its potential and limitations in the next chapter. Let's dive deeper into what AI can—and can't—do.

CHAPTER 2: UNDERSTANDING AI'S POTENTIAL AND LIMITATIONS

What AI Can Do

Artificial intelligence has become one of the most transformative technologies of our time. It's hard to find a field or aspect of daily life that hasn't been influenced by AI in some way. From simplifying tasks to solving complex problems, AI's capabilities are vast and continually evolving. Let's explore what AI can do, focusing on its role in problem-solving, automation, and creativity.

Problem-Solving and Decision-Making

At its core, AI excels at problem-solving. It's designed to analyze vast amounts of data, identify patterns, and draw conclusions faster than any human. This capability makes AI an indispensable tool for decision-making across various scenarios, from healthcare to business operations.

Take healthcare, for example. AI-powered systems can scan medical records and imaging data to spot early signs of diseases like cancer. These systems don't just look for obvious markers; they analyze subtle patterns that even experienced doctors might miss. This ability to find the needle in the haystack can save lives by detecting conditions before they become critical.

In business, AI plays a crucial role in optimizing operations. A retail company might use AI to predict inventory needs by analyzing past sales trends, seasonal patterns, and even weather forecasts. This ensures shelves are stocked with the right products at the right time, reducing waste and boosting customer satisfaction.

Even in personal finance, AI-driven tools help individuals make smarter decisions. Budgeting apps, for instance, analyze spending habits and offer tailored advice on how to save more effectively. These tools take the guesswork out of financial planning, empowering users to make informed choices.

Automation and Efficiency

One of AI's most practical benefits is its ability to automate repetitive tasks, freeing up time and resources for more meaningful work. Automation isn't just about convenience; it's about transforming industries and making them more efficient.

In manufacturing, AI-powered robots take on tasks like assembly, quality control, and even packaging. These machines don't tire or make mistakes from boredom, resulting in faster production times and higher-quality products. For example, car manufacturers use AI to inspect parts for defects with precision that surpasses human ability, ensuring safety and reliability.

In the office, AI streamlines workflows by automating administrative tasks. Virtual assistants can schedule meetings, sort emails, and even draft basic reports. This enables employees to focus on creative problem-solving and strategic planning instead of routine chores.

Even customer service has been revolutionized by AI automation. Chatbots handle basic inquiries around the clock, offering quick resolutions to common issues. These bots learn and improve over time, delivering more accurate and helpful responses as they gain experience. This not only saves businesses money but also enhances the customer experience by reducing wait times.

Advancing Creativity and Innovation

AI's ability to enhance creativity is one of its most surprising and exciting contributions. While creativity is often seen as uniquely human, AI is proving to be a powerful collaborator in fields like art, music, writing, and design.

In the world of art, AI tools like generative algorithms allow artists to experiment with styles and techniques in ways that were previously impossible. For example, an artist can input a basic concept into an AI program, which then generates multiple variations based on that idea. The artist can refine these outputs, merging their vision with the AI's suggestions to create something entirely new.

Music composition has also been transformed by

AI. Tools like Amper Music enable musicians to create custom tracks by choosing parameters such as mood, genre, and tempo. AI takes these inputs and composes original music, which can serve as a starting point or even a finished product for films, ads, or personal projects. Musicians are no longer constrained by technical skills or resources—they can let their imagination lead while AI handles the execution.

In writing, AI tools assist authors and marketers in brainstorming ideas, crafting outlines, and even generating content. These tools don't replace human creativity; instead, they act as catalysts, sparking inspiration and speeding up the creative process. For instance, a copywriter might use AI to draft multiple versions of an ad slogan, selecting the one that resonates most with their audience.

AI's creative potential extends beyond the arts. In industries like architecture and engineering, AI helps professionals design more efficient and sustainable buildings. By analyzing factors such as energy usage, materials, and environmental impact, AI provides insights that drive innovation forward, making designs both practical and groundbreaking.

AI's capabilities are vast, spanning problem-solving, automation, and creativity. It empowers professionals to make smarter decisions, handle tasks more efficiently, and push the boundaries of innovation. As remarkable as these abilities are, they represent only part of the picture. In the next section, we'll explore what AI cannot do—its limitations and the challenges it faces in replicating human intelligence. Understanding both sides of the story is essential for a balanced perspective on this transformative technology.

What AI Cannot Do (Yet)

As powerful and impressive as AI is, it's not without its limitations. While AI excels at processing data, identifying patterns, and even aiding in creative endeavors, there are areas where it falls short. AI is far from replicating human intelligence in its entirety, and understanding these limitations helps us set realistic expectations and use AI responsibly. Let's explore three key areas where AI struggles: understanding like humans, dependence on human input, and long-term challenges.

AI's Limitations in Understanding

AI can process vast amounts of data at incredible speeds, but it lacks the ability to truly understand or reason like humans do. For instance, an AI system might generate a detailed summary of a news article, but it doesn't grasp the emotional or social nuances within the content. It doesn't "know" what the story means or why it matters, it simply identifies patterns and produces an output based on its training.

One of AI's biggest challenges is its lack of common sense. Humans intuitively understand that an umbrella is needed when it's raining or that a glass of water shouldn't be placed near the edge of a table. AI, however, doesn't possess this type of innate knowledge. It can only "learn" what it's explicitly trained to recognize. This limitation means that AI can sometimes produce results that are technically correct but lack practical or logical coherence.

Emotional intelligence is another area where AI falls short. While AI can simulate empathy in customer service chatbots or virtual assistants, it doesn't genuinely "feel" or understand emotions. Its responses are programmed to mimic human interaction, but the underlying connection isn't there. This limitation becomes particularly apparent in contexts where emotional depth and nuance are essential, such as counseling or creative storytelling.

Dependence on Human Input

AI may seem autonomous, but it heavily relies on humans for direction, guidance, and data. Without quality input, AI systems can't function effectively. Every AI model begins with a dataset—information curated, labeled, and prepared by humans. If this data is flawed, incomplete, or biased, the resulting AI system will reflect those shortcomings.

For instance, an AI system designed to screen job applications can only be as fair as the data it's trained on. If historical hiring practices were biased against certain groups, the AI may unintentionally perpetuate those biases. This reliance on human-provided data highlights the critical role we play in shaping AI's performance and impact.

Moreover, AI systems require human oversight to make ethical decisions. In scenarios like autonomous driving, AI can process environmental data to avoid collisions, but complex moral decisions—such as prioritizing one life over another in an unavoidable accident—remain beyond its reach. These ethical dilemmas underline the importance of human involvement in guiding AI applications.

Even in creative fields, where AI tools generate art or music, human input is key. Artists and creators provide initial prompts, refine outputs, and make final decisions. AI serves as an assistant, not a replacement, relying on human judgment to bring projects to life.

Long-Term Challenges

While AI has made remarkable strides, there are long-term challenges that limit its capabilities. One significant hurdle is energy consumption. Training large AI models requires immense computational power, which translates to high energy use. This raises concerns about the environmental impact of AI development, especially as demand for more advanced systems grows. Making AI more energy-efficient is a priority for researchers and developers.

Another challenge is scalability. While AI can handle specific tasks exceptionally well, applying its capabilities across diverse environments is complex. For example, an AI trained to recognize faces in one cultural context may struggle to perform accurately in another due to differences in features, expressions, or lighting conditions. Adapting AI for global applications requires careful consideration of these variations.

Finally, the rapid pace of AI evolution creates its own set of challenges. As new algorithms, tools, and systems emerge, keeping them secure and preventing misuse becomes increasingly important. AI's potential to generate deepfakes or manipulate information has already shown how powerful tools can be used for harmful purposes. Addressing these risks requires not only technological innovation but also strong governance and ethical standards.

Understanding what AI cannot do is just as important as appreciating what it can achieve. Its limitations in understanding, reliance on human input, and long-term challenges remind us that AI, for all its power, remains a tool. It's a tool that can amplify human potential but cannot replace the depth of human thought, emotion, and ethical reasoning. By recognizing these boundaries, we can use AI more effectively and responsibly, ensuring it serves as a complement to, rather than a substitute for, human intelligence. Next, we'll explore the ethical considerations and risks associated with AI, a crucial aspect of navigating its growing role in our lives.

CHAPTER 3: GETTING STARTED WITH AI TOOLS

Choosing the Right AI Tools

N ow that you have a foundational understanding of what AI is, how it works, and its potential, the next step is incorporating it into your daily life or work. With so many AI tools available, it can feel overwhelming to know where to start. The key is to choose tools that align with your needs, whether for personal productivity, creative projects, or professional tasks. In this section, we'll explore the differences between free and paid AI tools, highlight some popular tools for personal use, and discuss options tailored for professional environments.

Free vs. Paid AI Tools

One of the first decisions you'll face is whether to use free or paid AI tools. Both have their advantages, and the right choice depends on your goals, budget, and how you plan to use the tool.

Free AI tools are a fantastic starting point, especially if you're new to AI and want to experiment without financial commitment. Many of these tools offer robust features, allowing you to explore what's possible. For example, tools like Google Translate or Grammarly's basic version provide powerful functionality at no cost. These tools can help you understand the basics of AI-powered productivity and make simple tasks more efficient.

Paid tools, on the other hand, often come with advanced features, better support, and greater customization options. They're designed for users who need professional-grade capabilities or plan to use AI extensively. For instance, tools like Adobe Photoshop's AI-enhanced features or Jasper AI for content creation offer advanced options that free versions can't match. If your work involves complex projects or specific needs, investing in a paid tool might be worth it.

The choice between free and paid tools isn't always black and white. Many paid tools offer free trials or basic plans, so you can try them before committing. If you're just starting, a good approach is to explore free options first and then transition to paid tools as your needs and confidence grow.

Tools for Personal Productivity

AI tools can significantly enhance how you organize your life, manage your time, and accomplish tasks more efficiently. Whether you're balancing work, family, or personal projects, there's likely an AI tool that can help simplify your day.

For notetaking and organization, tools like Notion and Evernote integrate AI to help you categorize and retrieve information effortlessly. You can use these tools to keep track of ideas, plan projects, or even collaborate with others. AI features like automatic tagging and smart search save time and make finding what you need a breeze.

If you're trying to stay on top of daily tasks, AI-powered virtual assistants like Google Assistant or Apple's Siri can act as your personal organizer. These tools can set reminders, schedule meetings, and answer quick questions, helping you stay focused and productive. They integrate seamlessly with your devices, ensuring your day runs smoothly without constant manual input.

AI tools for health and wellness are also gaining popularity. Apps like MyFitnessPal use AI to track your diet and exercise, providing personalized recommendations to help you achieve your goals. Sleep apps analyze your patterns and offer insights to improve your rest. These tools take the guesswork out of self-care, enabling you to make informed choices for a healthier lifestyle.

Tools for Professional Use

In the workplace, AI tools are transforming how we approach tasks, collaborate with teams, and achieve goals. Whether you're a freelancer, an entrepreneur, or part of a larger organization, there are AI tools designed to enhance your professional life.

For project management, platforms like Trello and Asana integrate AI to streamline workflows. They help prioritize tasks, set deadlines, and monitor progress, ensuring your team stays on track. AI features like automated reminders and predictive analytics make managing complex projects more efficient.

Marketing professionals can leverage AI tools like HubSpot or Canva Pro for content creation and audience engagement. These platforms analyze data to suggest the best times to post, create targeted campaigns, and even generate visuals or copy. With AI handling repetitive tasks, marketers can focus on strategy and creativity.

Customer engagement is another area where AI shines. Chatbots powered by AI, such as Zendesk or Intercom, handle customer inquiries 24/7, providing quick resolutions to common issues. These tools not only improve customer satisfaction but also free up human agents to tackle more complex problems.

AI tools tailored for professional use are designed to maximize efficiency, creativity, and impact. Whether you're automating repetitive tasks or gaining insights from data, the right tools can make a significant difference in your work.

Choosing the right AI tools can feel daunting at first, but it's all about finding what works for you. By understanding the trade-offs between free and paid options, exploring tools for personal productivity, and leveraging professional-grade platforms, you can unlock the true potential of AI. In the next section, we'll guide you through learning AI step by step, helping you build the confidence to use these tools effectively in your everyday life. Let's get started!

Learning AI Step by Step

Diving into AI for the first time can feel overwhelming, especially if you're not particularly tech-savvy. The good news is that learning AI doesn't require a computer science degree or advanced technical skills. With the right approach, you can build your knowledge step by step, gaining confidence along the way. This section breaks down the learning process into three manageable parts: experimenting with user-friendly tools, building basic AI models, and staying updated with advancements.

Experimenting with User-Friendly AI Apps

The easiest way to start learning about AI is by experimenting with user-friendly tools that don't require any coding or technical expertise. These tools are designed with beginners in mind, making it easy to understand the basics of how AI works while seeing its practical applications in action.

For example, you might start with a tool like ChatGPT or DALL-E, which allows you to interact with AI conversationally or create stunning visuals from simple text prompts. Playing around with these tools is not only fun but also an excellent way to grasp AI's capabilities and limitations. You'll quickly learn how AI responds to the instructions you give it and how it processes information to generate results.

Another great entry point is experimenting with voice assistants like Siri, Alexa, or Google Assistant. Try asking them complex questions, giving them tasks, or having them organize your day. This will help you understand how natural language processing works—the part of AI that enables machines to interpret and respond to human speech.

If you're curious about how AI handles images, try tools like Canva's AI design features or photo editing apps like Luminar AI. These platforms let you enhance photos or create graphics with minimal effort, giving you a firsthand look at how AI can simplify creative tasks.

The goal here isn't to master AI right away but to explore and familiarize yourself with its capabilities. Think of these tools as a sandbox where you can experiment and learn without any pressure.

Building Basic AI Models

Once you're comfortable with user-friendly tools, you might feel ready to take things a step further by building basic AI models. Don't worry, this doesn't mean diving into complex programming. Today, there are no-code or low-code platforms that make creating simple AI models accessible to almost anyone.

Platforms like Google's Teachable Machine or Microsoft's Azure AI offer intuitive interfaces that guide you through the process of training a model. For instance, you could use Teachable Machine to create a model that recognizes different objects using your webcam. All you need to do is upload examples of each object, and the platform handles the rest. It's a hands-on way to see how AI learns from data.

If you're interested in text-based AI, tools like RunwayML allow you to experiment with pre-built AI templates for tasks like generating captions or summarizing text. These platforms show you the behind-the-scenes process of how data is fed into an algorithm, how the model trains on that data, and how it applies what it has learned.

The purpose of building basic models isn't to become a data scientist overnight; it's to deepen your understanding of AI's inner workings. By creating something simple, you'll gain a better appreciation for the process of training, testing, and refining AI systems. It also demystifies the technology, making it feel less like magic and more like a set of logical steps.

Staying Updated with AI Advancements

AI is a rapidly evolving field, with new tools, techniques, and breakthroughs emerging all the time. Staying informed about these developments is key to growing your AI knowledge and making the most of what the technology offers.

Start by following trusted AI news sources like MIT Technology Review, Wired, or specialized websites like OpenAI's blog. These outlets break down complex topics into digestible insights, helping you stay updated without feeling overwhelmed. Social media platforms and YouTube channels focused on tech education are also great resources for bite-sized updates.

Joining AI communities and forums can also be incredibly beneficial. Platforms like Reddit, Stack Overflow, or even LinkedIn groups dedicated to AI provide opportunities to ask questions, share experiences, and learn from others. Engaging with a community keeps you motivated and gives you access to real-world applications and advice from people with varying levels of expertise.

Finally, consider taking online AI courses tailored for beginners. Websites like Coursera, Udemy, and TheAiVilleExpert.com offer classes that cover everything from AI basics to more advanced topics like machine learning and data science. These courses often include interactive projects, allowing you to apply what you've learned in a practical setting.

The world of AI is always changing, but by staying curious and proactive, you'll keep building on the knowledge you've gained. Learning AI step by step isn't just about mastering technology, it's about developing the confidence to explore, experiment, and apply AI in ways that matter to you.

Learning AI doesn't have to be intimidating. By experimenting with easy-to-use tools, building basic models, and staying engaged with the latest developments, you'll set yourself on a path to becoming AI-savvy. In the next section, we'll explore how to take this newfound knowledge and apply it to real-world scenarios, helping you make AI a meaningful part of your personal and professional life. Let's put your learning into action!

Applying AI Knowledge

Now that you've explored AI tools and taken your first steps in learning how they work, it's time to put your newfound knowledge into action. AI becomes most valuable when it's integrated into your daily life, whether that's solving problems at work, pursuing personal projects, or managing your day-to-day responsibilities. This section focuses on applying AI knowledge to work-related challenges, personalizing it for creative endeavors, and creating a roadmap for your long-term growth with AI.

Solving Work-Related Challenges with AI

AI can transform how you approach work, offering smarter solutions to common challenges and streamlining processes to free up time for more meaningful tasks. To start, think about the repetitive or time-consuming tasks in your job—these are often perfect candidates for AI automation. For instance, if you frequently analyze data, AI tools like Tableau or Microsoft Power BI can generate insights in minutes, saving you hours of manual effort. These tools help identify trends, predict outcomes, and visualize data in a way that's easy to understand and share with your team.

If your work involves managing a team or collaborating on projects, AI-powered platforms like Asana or Slack can keep everyone on the same page. AI can prioritize tasks, flag deadlines, and even suggest ways to improve workflow efficiency. This means fewer meetings and less time spent sorting out miscommunications, allowing your team to focus on the work that truly matters.

AI is also incredibly helpful for decision-making. Tools like IBM Watson or Salesforce Einstein analyze large datasets and provide recommendations, helping you make informed choices. For example, a sales manager could use AI to identify which leads are most likely to convert, optimizing resources and boosting revenue. By applying AI strategically, you can tackle complex problems with greater confidence and efficiency.

Personalizing Projects with AI

AI isn't just for work, it's also a powerful tool for personal projects, hobbies, and creative pursuits. Whether you're a writer, artist, or entrepreneur, AI can amplify your creativity and help bring your ideas to life.

For writers, AI tools like Jasper or Grammarly can help you brainstorm ideas, refine your drafts, or generate content based on your prompts. This is particularly useful if you're tackling a large project like a novel or blog series, as AI can provide suggestions to keep your ideas flowing. You're still the creator, but AI acts as your collaborative assistant, offering insights and inspiration.

For visual artists and designers, tools like Canva or Adobe Firefly simplify the creative process. Whether you're designing social media graphics, creating a logo for your small business, or experimenting with digital art, AI can speed up your workflow while allowing you to explore new styles and concepts. The beauty of AI in creative projects is that it empowers you to experiment without fear—if you don't like the output, you can always tweak it or start over.

Even for personal development projects, AI can be a game-changer. If you're learning a new language, tools like Duolingo use AI to adapt lessons to your pace and preferences. If you're into fitness, apps like Fitbit and MyFitnessPal leverage AI to tailor recommendations for your goals. These tools make learning and self-improvement more accessible, keeping you motivated and engaged.

Creating a Personal AI Growth Plan

To make the most of your AI knowledge, it's essential to have a plan. Think of this as your roadmap for integrating AI into your personal and professional life. Start by identifying the areas where AI can have the greatest impact. For example, if your work involves a lot of data analysis, focus on mastering AI tools that specialize in that area. If you're a creative professional, explore platforms that enhance your artistic or writing skills.

Set achievable goals to guide your learning. Maybe you want to automate a specific task at work within the next month, or perhaps you're aiming to use AI to launch a side project within six months. Breaking down these goals into smaller, actionable steps makes them less intimidating and more attainable.

As part of your growth plan, commit to staying curious and open to new advancements. AI evolves rapidly, and keeping up with the latest tools and trends will ensure you remain ahead of the curve. Consider scheduling regular check-ins with yourself to assess your progress and explore new opportunities. Joining AI-focused communities or taking short online courses can also help you stay motivated and connected.

A personal AI growth plan isn't just about using AI —it's about thinking strategically and developing a mindset that embraces innovation. With the right approach, you'll not only deepen your expertise but also discover new ways to use AI that align with your goals and passions.

Applying AI knowledge is where the magic happens. By solving challenges at work, personalizing AI for your projects, and creating a growth plan, you'll turn what you've learned into tangible results. The more you integrate AI into your life, the more confident and empowered you'll become. In the next chapter, we'll explore how to approach AI responsibly, diving into the ethical considerations and risks that come with using this powerful technology. Let's ensure your journey with AI is both impactful and responsible

CONCLUSION: YOUR AI JOURNEY AHEAD

Congratulations! You've taken significant steps to demystify artificial intelligence, exploring what it is, how it works, and how it can fit into your life. AI is no longer a vague, intimidating concept; it's a tool you can use with confidence to solve problems, spark creativity, and make life a little easier. This conclusion will recap the key takeaways from your journey, encourage you to keep exploring, and leave you with a call to action as you step into the world of AI.

Recap of Key Takeaways

Think back to where you started. Perhaps you knew little about AI or felt unsure about how it applied to you. Now, you understand the basics of what AI is, a tool that uses data and algorithms to mimic certain aspects of human intelligence. You've explored its applications in everyday life, business, and specialized industries, realizing that AI is already a part of the world around you, from the apps on your phone to the innovations shaping healthcare and education.

You've learned how AI works, from the role of data to the mechanics of algorithms and the hardware that powers it. More importantly, you've seen what AI can and cannot do. It's not a replacement for human intelligence but a complement to it, amplifying our abilities while still relying on human oversight and guidance.

Finally, you've gained practical knowledge on how to use AI tools, learn step by step, and apply what you've learned to real-world scenarios. Whether automating repetitive tasks, personalizing creative projects, or planning your growth with AI, you now have the foundation to make AI a meaningful part of your life.

Encouragement to Keep Exploring

The journey doesn't end here. AI is constantly

evolving, and the possibilities it offers will only continue to grow. Staying curious is your most powerful tool. The more you explore, the more opportunities you'll uncover to use AI in ways that align with your goals and passions.

Think of AI as a toolbox rather than a single solution. Not every tool will be right for every job, and that's okay. The key is to experiment, adapt, and find what works best for you. Whether you're streamlining your workday, diving into a creative project, or solving a unique problem, there's likely an AI tool or approach that can help.

Don't be afraid to push boundaries. AI thrives on innovation, and as you gain confidence, you'll discover new ways to use it that others might not have considered. Join communities, share your experiences, and learn from others who are also navigating the AI landscape.

A Call to Action

Now it's time to take what you've learned and put it into action. Choose one area of your life where AI could make an immediate impact. Perhaps it's automating a tedious task, exploring a new creative

tool, or enhancing your decision-making at work. Start small, experiment, and let your curiosity guide you.

As you explore, remember that AI isn't just about technology, it's about what you can achieve with it. Share your discoveries with friends, colleagues, or online communities. The more we collectively understand AI, the more we can use it responsibly and effectively.

Your journey with AI is just beginning. The knowledge and confidence you've gained from this book are your steppingstones to a world of possibilities. So go ahead, explore, innovate, and create. The

future of AI is bright, and you're now equipped to be part of it. Let's see what you'll achieve!

THEAIVILLEEXPERT.COM

An excellent way to continue your journey is by joining a dynamic community of AI enthusiasts, just like you. To discover *"The Place for People Who Love AI,"* follow "TheAiVilleExpert.com, where everything AI is at your fingertips. It's a chance to connect with others who share your passion for AI and gain insights that will propel your AI journey forward.

Thank You...

I want to thank you for reading this book. If you have found this to be of value, it would mean a lot to me if you could leave a review on Amazon. I would love to hear from you. Meanwhile, I wish you the very best.

References

Software and Platforms:

Adobe Firefly. (n.d.). AI-enhanced creative design tool. Retrieved from https://www.adobe.com

Adobe Photoshop. (n.d.). AI-powered design and editing features. Retrieved from https://www.adobe.com/photoshop

Asana. (n.d.). Project management platform with AI features. Retrieved from https://www.asana.com

Azure AI. (n.d.). AI development platform by Microsoft. Retrieved from https://azure.microsoft.com/en-us/services/machine-learning

Canva. (n.d.). AI-powered design tools. Retrieved from https://www.canva.com

ChatGPT. (n.d.). OpenAI conversational AI tool. Retrieved from https://chat.openai.com

DALL-E. (n.d.). AI-powered visual generation tool. Retrieved from https://openai.com/dall-e

Duolingo. (n.d.). AI-driven language

learning platform. Retrieved from https://www.duolingo.com

Fitbit. (n.d.). AI in fitness tracking. Retrieved from https://www.fitbit.com

Google Assistant. (n.d.). Personal productivity assistant by Google. Retrieved from https://assistant.google.com

Google Translate. (n.d.). AI-based language translation tool. Retrieved from https://translate.google.com

Grammarly. (n.d.). AI-powered writing assistance. Retrieved from https://www.grammarly.com

HubSpot. (n.d.). AI-driven marketing platform. Retrieved from https://www.hubspot.com

BM Watson. (n.d.). AI for decision-making and analytics. Retrieved from https://www.ibm.com/watson

Jasper. (n.d.). AI content creation tool. Retrieved from https://www.jasper.ai

Luminar AI. (n.d.). AI-powered photo editing software. Retrieved from https://skylum.com/luminar

Microsoft Power BI. (n.d.). AI-driven data analysis tool. Retrieved from https://powerbi.microsoft.com

MyFitnessPal. (n.d.). AI-based health tracking application. Retrieved from https://www.myfitnesspal.com

Notion. (n.d.). AI-supported productivity and organization platform. Retrieved from https://www.notion.so

RunwayML. (n.d.). AI tool for creative projects. Retrieved from https://runwayml.com

Salesforce Einstein. (n.d.). AI platform for business decision-making. Retrieved from https://www.salesforce.com/products/einstein

Slack. (n.d.). AI-enhanced team collaboration tool. Retrieved from https://slack.com

Tableau. (n.d.). Data analysis with AI capabilities. Retrieved from https://www.tableau.com

Teachable Machine. (n.d.). Beginner-friendly platform for building AI models. Retrieved from https://teachablemachine.withgoogle.com

Trello. (n.d.). Project management tool with AI features. Retrieved from https://trello.com

Udemy. (n.d.). Online courses for AI education. Retrieved from https://www.udemy.com

Zendesk. (n.d.). AI-powered customer service platform. Retrieved from https://www.zendesk.com

Publications and Blogs:

MIT Technology Review. (n.d.). Trusted source for AI-related news. Retrieved from https://www.technologyreview.com

OpenAI Blog. (n.d.). Updates and resources on AI advancements. Retrieved from https://openai.com/blog

Wired. (n.d.). Technology and AI updates. Retrieved from https://www.wired.com

Educational Resources:

Coursera. (n.d.). *CourseRA | Degrees, Certificates, & free online courses.* https://www.coursera.org/

Khan Academy. (n.d.). Educational resources for AI and technology. Retrieved from https://www.khanacademy.org

Stack Overflow. (n.d.). Learning and discussion

platform for AI and programming. Retrieved from https://stackoverflow.com